The Return of the Wolf

Margaret Su
Illustrated by Bradley Clark

A Harcourt Achieve Imprint

www.Rigby.com
1-800-531-5015

For my Nibler pack—Jeff, Max, and Calvin

Literacy by Design Leveled Readers: *The Return of the Wolf*

ISBN-13: 978-1-4189-3921-2
ISBN-10: 1-4189-3921-8

Printed in China
1 2 3 4 5 6 7 8 985 13 12 11 10 09 08 07 06

Contents

Chapter 1

Lone Wolf

Wen Zhang was not alone. Others from his pack ran beside him as they rushed through the forest of darkened treetops and cold stone. The distant mountains cast a ragged shadow over the valley floor, like a silent vulture hovering over its prey.

A crack of thunder broke through the sky. It was followed by a long, mournful howl. Wen realized that the howl was his. He ran as fast as his four legs could take him, but he couldn't keep up with the rest of the pack. As lightning crashed all around him, the others were getting further and further ahead. Soon they were gone completely, and Wen let out another howl, the cry of a lone wolf. Thunder struck again, shattering everything.

And with a jerk of his head, Wen woke from his dream.

Jing Zhang smiled at her son from the driver's seat. "Hey, sleepyhead. That must have been some dream. You sounded like you were barking."

"I was dreaming about wolves," Wen said.

"Soon you'll be doing more than just dreaming about them."

Wen stared out at the deep green trees rushing past his window. "Mom, what are wolves like? Are they dangerous?"

Jing shook her head. "Wolves are wild animals, which means we need to keep our distance. But they also have a natural fear of humans, so they aren't likely to get close to us."

Then she patted his knee. "Aren't you excited, Wen? We get to spend two weeks observing the wolves of Yellowstone National Park!"

"Oh sure," Wen answered with a weak smile. "I'm totally excited."

Jing slowed the car as they approached a stone arch marking the entrance to Yellowstone National Park. As they passed under the arch, Wen read the inscription on its face:

For the Benefit and Enjoyment of the People

"I guess there's no turning back now," Wen sighed to himself.

A sinking feeling settled into the pit of his stomach. He'd never really been on a trip like this before. Would he be able to carry his own weight? Would he be of any use to the team? He'd never been much good at anything, except reading. And what good would that do, he wondered gloomily as they drove past amazing views of mountainous canyons and wide valleys. Yellowstone National Park was 2.5 million acres of wild and scary forest, and Wen felt very far from the familiar city he called home.

Chapter 2

New Friends

The first person Wen and Jing met after arriving at the campsite was Tae-Song Chang. Tae-Song was a naturalist for the Yellowstone park service and would be the leader of their group. He had a friendly tone in his voice that put Wen a bit more at ease.

A woman with a notepad and a pen stuck behind her ear came up to them next. "I'm Josephine Simon, nature writer. Pleased to meet you. This is my daughter Gina."

Gina shook Wen's hand as though she were a professional businessperson shaking the hand of another businessperson. "Pleased to meet you, Wen. Name's Gina. I'm a writer like my mom. What do you do?"

Wen hesitated, then replied, "Nothing. I just came to help."

Gina eyed him with a sideways look as if to say, *What can you do to help?*

Tae-Song pointed at the man standing next to him. "This is Luis Ramos, our wildlife veterinarian and wolf expert. And this is his son Pepe."

"Hi! Where are you from?" Pepe asked in a friendly, easy manner. But before Wen could even answer, Pepe quickly answered himself, "I heard you're from southern California. That's cool. My family lives on a farm in Idaho, so we live pretty close to here. Have you ever been on a trip like this before, Wen?"

Wen shook his head. "Not really."

"But it's pretty cool, huh?" Pepe continued. "I mean, I can't wait to get unpacked and go exploring!"

Wen smiled the best he could so Pepe wouldn't see how anxious he really was.

"Your mom's a photographer?" Gina asked.

Wen nodded. "She's really excited, but she's also kind of nervous. We're from the city, so we haven't done much camping." He laughed uneasily. Even though he'd said *she*, what he really meant was *me*.

Gina replied, "I'm not nervous. I've been on tons of nature writing assignments. I just hope everyone knows what to do. I mean, the chain's only as strong as its weakest link."

Wen wondered why Gina stared at him while she said this.

Pepe spoke up in his chatty manner, "Anyway, we're all here to help if you need it. I remember this one time, I tore a hole in my tent because I didn't know what I was doing. I didn't let it bother me. Camping is supposed to be fun!"

Gina shrugged and walked away to unpack the rest of her writing journals and pens. Pepe ignored her as she left, but Wen was afraid she might be right. He could be their weakest link.

"This stuff about the wolves is cool, huh?" Pepe asked. Too quick to wait for a reply, he answered himself excitedly, "I love wolves, but I've never seen a real one. Have you? I bet you have."

Wen shook his head and said, "I've actually only read about them." He didn't want to bore Pepe with a discussion on all the wolf books he'd read, though he certainly could have. He'd read a ton.

Pepe added, "The wolves were wiped out of this area because people were afraid of them and thought they were, you know, really dangerous."

He called his father Luis over. "My dad's been helping the park service bring wolves back to Yellowstone."

Wen frowned thoughtfully. "So, Mr. Ramos, if people are afraid of the wolves, why'd they bring them back?"

"Because the wolves are important to the park," Luis answered. "We've learned that other animals depend on them for survival."

"Like how?" Wen and Pepe asked at the same time.

"Well, that's what we're here to discover," Luis said with a grin. "We'll videotape, photograph, and document the effects the wolves have on the park."

Pepe beamed, "We're here to find out what's happened since the return of the wolf!"

Wen couldn't help but smile along with his new friend.

Chapter 3

Overconfident

Setting up the camp was an adventure in itself. Pepe seemed like a natural at camping. He moved around the camp with ease. His tent was assembled lickety-split, and he ran off to explore a nearby stream. Gina had apparently memorized the camping guidelines, because she went around making sure everyone followed the rules. Wen, meanwhile, struggled with his tent. Jing came over to help as soon as she'd unpacked their clothes and gear.

When it was Gina's turn to put up her tent, Wen was glad to see that she struggled as much as he had. Apparently Gina didn't know everything about everything. She refused everyone's help—right up until she slammed her thumb with the hammer while trying to drive a stake into the ground.

"Gina seems nice," Jing said, tying down the last cord on Wen's tent. "But she needs to learn to work with the team, not against it. We're all in this together, and we'll need everyone if this mission is going to be a success."

A short while later, Wen wandered over to help Pepe and Gina set up the chemistry table Tae-Song was going to use to study the plant samples the teams would collect during their stay. There were Petri dishes for growing molds and fungus, a microscope for looking at leaf cells, and test tubes to hold the soil samples that Tae-Song wanted to take back to his lab.

As the kids set up the equipment, Gina impatiently pointed out places where Wen could do things better. Either he was going too slowly, or too fast. He didn't seem to be doing anything right. Wen felt even more unsure of himself.

As Gina lifted a heavy cardboard box filled with equipment, the bottom of the box gave out, and everything began to fall to the ground. Gina gasped, but there was nothing she could do.

Luckily, Wen's reflexes were quick. He dove and saved the microscope from certain destruction.

15

Pepe also acted fast. He caught a stack of Petri dishes in one hand and a bunch of test tubes in the other. He could barely manage to keep his balance as he tried to keep from falling over Wen.

For a moment no one dared to breathe.

Then, Pepe and Wen began to laugh, both amused and amazed at what had just happened. They looked like some kind of strange statue.

Finally Wen stood up, brushed himself off, and put the microscope on the table. "Nice save, Pepe."

Pepe grinned back, "You, too."

Gina was not laughing. Instead, she was flushed and upset with herself. "I am so sorry! The box was too heavy, and I shouldn't have picked it up by myself!"

Pepe shrugged. "Accidents happen."

"Especially to me!" Wen chuckled and, finally, so did Gina.

After dinner, Wen overheard Josephine speaking to Gina. "I know you were only trying to help, but you try to do too much on your own. This trip is about teamwork. Gathering information on the wolves will be tricky. The only way our project will be a success is if we all work together."

Chapter 4

The Lookout Spot

To Wen, Yellowstone National Park seemed like a bewildering mess of unknown trees, strange shrubs, and countless rocks. Being from the city, he was used to finding his way around using street signs and landmarks, but nothing in this new environment even came close to a building or a lamp post. Everything here looked the same, and he couldn't seem to remember where he'd first seen something or what type of plant he was looking at.

Frustrated with always feeling lost, Wen decided to do something about it. He had stashed away a few plant books in his backpack to take with him on hikes. While Pepe and Gina rested, Wen flipped through the books. He studied his surroundings, taking note of important details. Soon, he began to recognize plants he'd seen before. He even knew their names.

After looking up the trees in his books, he could tell the different species apart by their markings, the shapes of their leaves or needles, and the color of their bark. He took note of interesting landmarks, like a castle-shaped log or a comfortable rock near the stream.

Gina and Pepe would watch him studying his books. When they asked what he was doing, Wen had a simple answer for them: "Nothing."

Their camp was located one mile from a lookout spot that was perfect for watching out for wolves. They had yet to see any actual wolves, but Tae-Song assured them that the project was just getting heated up.

Every morning, Tae-Song took Wen, Pepe, and Gina up to the lookout spot while the rest of the group watched the northern edge of the forest. They were sure to get a glimpse of something from up there.

"Wolves mostly travel in packs," Tae-Song informed the kids, "though sometimes you might come across a lone wolf. That's a wolf that has either chosen to live on its own, or it has been forced to."

"Why would a wolf be forced out of the pack?" Wen asked as the group followed the rugged path up to the lookout spot.

"Sometimes the pack's leader doesn't want competition from other males. Or maybe the wolf is weak or old and therefore a danger to the pack's survival. The pack might leave it behind."

The rocky incline up to the point was not too steep or dangerous, but the loose rocks made it a challenge.

Pepe shot up to the top with no trouble at all, but Wen and Gina took their time, occasionally helped by Tae-Song. Wen showed Gina footholds and handholds he'd spotted that made the climb easier.

At the top Gina gave him a shy, but grateful, smile. "Thanks."

"No problem," Wen replied.

They'd arrived at a wide clearing where the valley floor spread out in waves of color. The scene was bordered by majestic mountain peaks and a rich blue sky. The air smelled clean and crisp. *Not a building or lamp post in sight*, Wen thought as a lonely leaf blew by.

"We're here because the Pine Creek pack sometimes travels through this area," Tae-Song explained. "But don't expect to see the wolves right away. They aren't going to just walk right up to us."

Wen noticed that Pepe was sitting far back from the edge, looking pale. "Are you okay?" Wen asked.

"I-I d-don't like heights," Pepe stammered. "Don't tell anyone, OK?"

"But you climbed up here so fast!"

"I'm a good climber. I'm just afraid of heights."

Wen patted his friend on the shoulder. "Don't worry. Your secret's safe with me."

Gina jumped up suddenly and pointed. "Wolf!" she whispered loudly, but not too loudly that she'd scare it away.

Everyone rushed forward to see.

Tae-Song gazed to where she was pointing. "I'm afraid that's just a coyote. They have a similar look, but coyotes are more closely related to dogs than wolves."

Wen thought Gina would be angry at being corrected. Instead, she began asking Tae-Song questions about the coyote. Wen had noticed that she'd been much nicer lately on their hikes. Also, she'd stopped telling everyone what to do.

Pepe whispered to Wen, "You know, at first I kind of thought Gina was mean, but now I'm starting to think she might be cool."

Chapter 5

A Place in the Pack

Over the next few days, Wen grew bolder, exploring further from camp. He was becoming more comfortable with the sights and sounds of the wilderness. With so many things to examine and learn about, it was easy to forget that they hadn't yet seen a single wolf.

One afternoon, Tae-Song took the three of them out to study the Yellowstone ecosystem. He explained that an ecosystem is the way plants and animals in an environment live together and depend on each other.

"The willow and aspen trees," Tae-Song said, "are only just beginning to return to this area. While the wolves were gone, the elk population grew very large and were eating all the bark off the trees. This killed a lot of trees, which in turn hurt the animals that depend on the trees, such as beavers and birds."

Gina chewed the tip of her pen thoughtfully.

"So in other words, a healthy ecosystem is all about balance. The wolves thin the elk population, which then helps the trees and animals."

"Animals like these ravens that build their nests in the trees," Pepe added, pointing to a group of dark birds perched in a nearby tree.

"Exactly!" Tae-Song cheered.

Gina jotted these notes into her journal for later. Pepe continued watching the ravens walk up and down the tree branch.

As for Wen, he sat off to the side, feeling out of place. He wasn't a writer like Gina. And he didn't know very much about animals like Pepe. Just as he'd feared, he was the one person struggling to find a useful place on the team.

A short while later, Wen noticed Pepe searching all around the forest floor. "Has anybody seen my canteen?"

Wen pointed to a patch of nearby plants and flowers. "It's over there."

"Over where?"

Wen continued to point. "It's over there in that patch of coralroots and harebells."

"Patch of what and what?" Gina asked.

Wen walked over to the flowers. "See? The coralroots have a leafless, yellow orchid flower.

And the harebells have a bell-shaped blue flower that's perennial, meaning it blooms all year long."

Pepe and Gina stared at Wen in wonder.

"That was amazing!" Pepe exclaimed. "How'd you do that?"

"Do what?" Wen asked.

Gina added, "I never would have seen that canteen in all those flowers."

Wen found himself smiling as wide as he was able. "I guess I'm used to using landmarks to find my way around the city. Once I'd identified some of the plant species from my books, it was easy to find my way around out here. I just pay attention to the details."

Pepe patted Wen on the back. "We're going to have to start calling you eagle eye."

As the team packed up for the trip back to camp, Wen couldn't help but smile to himself. He'd felt better than he had since arriving at Yellowstone National Park. And he thought that he might just have a place on this team after all.

Chapter Six

Wolf Sighting

The next morning, the group once again set out for the lookout spot. Sunlight shone through the trees, sprinkling the path in a soft glow. Tae-Song applauded Wen's powers of observation when he found a patch of wild strawberries.

As they ate the delicate fruit, Wen scanned the area for other interesting things, but he only noted a large rock with a jagged split running down the middle of it. It would make a good climbing rock the next time they came by. He noticed more coralroot like they'd seen the day before. He also noted an eight-blossom paintbrush flower that looked just like its name.

Then suddenly, something caught Wen's eye. He backtracked a few steps to get a better look at an unusual mark in the dirt. He called to the others, his heart pounding in anticipation.

Tae-Song inspected the mark, then gasped. "You did it, Wen! This is a wolf print."

"That's our eagle eye!" Gina cheered.

The team searched the area, coming across a second wolf print and then a couple more.

Tae-Song thought for a minute. "This only appears to be one wolf, not a pack. We'll have to see if we spot any more."

They reached the lookout spot and settled down to watch. As usual Pepe hung back, preferring to observe from several feet away. However, he was the first to notice a line of movement in the distance.

Tae-Song peered through a pair of binoculars, beaming in delight. "The Pine Creek pack! And they're headed in the direction of Jing and the rest of the group. If they're lucky, they might be able to capture this on film."

Tae-Song radioed Jing with the location and direction the pack was headed. It was an exciting moment for everyone as they watched the long line of wolves cross the plains.

The wolves were not solid gray, as Wen had once thought. One of the wolves was black, and a couple of the others were mostly white. They were much bigger and broader than in the pictures in his books.

Gina said, "After this, I don't think I'll ever mistake a coyote for a wolf again. Look at the size of those guys!"

Once the wolves were out of sight, the group paused to record their personal observations. Gina did the writing, which she had the most skill at. She stopped to ask questions now and then so that she wouldn't miss a thing. Pepe noted several details he knew about animals and the way the wolves had behaved. Wen pointed out several things that helped Gina describe the plant life and other landmarks of the wolves' journey.

Chapter 7

The White Wolf

Later that day the group packed up their equipment for the hike back to camp. They had seen two coyotes, a group of elk, and two species of birds that had only recently returned to the area. This was of great importance since it was a sign that the ecosystem was returning to its natural balance.

Gina smiled at the group as they gathered their things. "I never thought I would learn so much on this trip. I really feel like we make a good team."

Wen and Pepe smiled back, full of the same sense of accomplishment and purpose. Wen thought back over the past week and all their days of observation and discovery. "I guess we're just another example of how creatures depend on each other. We're an ecosystem, too!"

Just then Wen saw some movement out of the corner of his eye that stopped him in his tracks. It was large and white, a hulking shape that made Wen's blood run cold. Pepe gasped. Gina stood as still as a statue.

Coming out from the trees was a lean, white wolf with spots of gray. It moved with steady steps, its gaze focused on a spot a short distance away.

It took Wen a moment to realize what it was that held the wolf's attention. An enormous black bear was coming out of the trees toward the wolf. Gina gripped Wen's arm in horror, her fingers digging painfully into his skin. Wen hardly noticed.

No one made a sound. Luckily, they were on a ledge out of the animals' reach. They were too far away to be in any danger, but the scene still held them breathless.

The wolf was tense and still, its tail twitching wildly. It crouched close to the ground, then leapt with a fierce growl, baring its dual fangs. The bear dodged the attack, and the wolf landed behind it. The two animals circled each other like boxers in a ring. They snarled and growled at each other—one was trespassing on the other's territory. This battle would not end until the enemy was driven away, or killed.

With a sudden turn, the wolf lunged at the bear. The bear slashed its deadly paw through the air and knocked the wolf to the ground.

The wolf hit the ground hard, and it did not get up.

The bear was about to attack again when Wen cried out in alarm, and the bear, hearing the cry, stopped. It paused to sniff the ground, perhaps smelling humans close by. It looked confused and frightened, and it turned and walked away, not even sparing a backward glance toward the fallen wolf.

The duel was over.

Tae-Song was both worried and amazed. "I . . . " He paused for breath. "I've never seen anything like that. I can't imagine what would cause the wolf to attack the bear, especially on its own. I wouldn't have thought it possible."

They scrambled down from the ledge. The bear was gone, but the wolf lay still, clearly unconscious. There was a bare patch of fur near its stomach where the bear had struck it. Tae-Song ordered them to stay back while he bent down to check on the wolf. He looked up, a very worried expression on his face.

Tae-Song said, "She's a female, and she's been badly injured."

Pepe quickly dug through his backpack, pulling out a walkie-talkie radio. "I'll call my dad. He's a veterinarian, so he'll know what to do."

Pepe pushed the button to radio back to camp, but the radio only picked up static. Pepe tried again, but there was still nothing.

Gina pulled her walkie-talkie out of her backpack. "I'll try my mother on a different channel."

But neither of the radios was able to get a strong enough signal to reach camp. There was some sort of interference blocking it.

Finally Tae-Song said, "There's nothing else we can do right now. Let's get back to camp. We'll send Pepe's father back for the wolf once we get there."

Chapter 8

The Storm

As Tae-Song rose from his position near the wolf, a sudden rumbling shook the forest. It sounded like a heavy hammer cracking the sky above.

"What was that?" Wen cried out in astonishment. Then his expression changed, his face showing that he knew the answer to his own question.

"Thunderstorm!" Gina yelled, as the first fat raindrops landed on their heads.

They had been told that thunderstorms could break out with shocking speed, but the team was still surprised by how fast it had come. They were staring up in bewilderment when a blaze of light filled the sky.

The lightning jarred them awake, and they hurriedly gathered their things. Tae-Song called out, "Hurry! We've got to get out of this clearing! Keep your heads down and move!"

They ran for the cover of the forest, knowing they might find safety in the thicket of tall trees. Thunder boomed again, sounding closer and more threatening. A minute later a flash of lightning blazed through the forest. A harsh crash followed, meaning that the lightning had struck something nearby. All Wen could do was run as fast as he could. He kept an eye on Pepe as they ran in the direction of the mountain face. He stumbled over a pile of rocks and ran through a cluster of wildflowers, keeping his head low and wiping the rain from his eyes.

"There!" Pepe called, his voice faint over the rush of wind.

With great relief, Wen spotted a small cave in the mountainside behind a group of trees. He tugged on Pepe's shirt and pointed toward it. Leaping inside, the two boys crouched down at the narrow entrance and turned to look for Tae-Song and Gina.

There was no sign of them. Both boys looked at each other in alarm. The rain was falling even harder now, and their attempts to call out to the others were lost in the noise of the storm.

Pepe said with confidence, "Tae-Song knows what he's doing. I'm sure he and Gina are fine."

They were drenched and starting to shiver. Pepe tried to radio the others but only received more static. "It must be the storm," he said. "That's why we couldn't reach the camp earlier."

It was then that something at the back of the cave caught Wen's eye. He saw movement back there in the dark. Several things moved, actually. The roof of the cave was very low, and a small hollow was carved in the dirt floor against the far wall. Resting comfortably inside the hollow were four small creatures. They were furry and light in color, and as Wen drew closer, he could see that the animals were asleep.

Wen blinked in the gloom, then turned to Pepe. "Do you see them?"

Pepe crouched down in wonder. "Wolf pups! I never thought I'd actually see some."

He looked over at Wen, his eyes wide in amazement. "We've stumbled into a wolf's den!"

Water from Wen's hair ran in cold trickles down his face, dripping onto the collar of his shirt. The pups lay in warm bundles, curled against each other in a gentle pile of fuzzy fur and musty puppy odor. Their plump bodies vibrated with the rhythm of each breath, lightly stirring the fur of their companions. Wen and Pepe watched in silence, both struck with a deep understanding of the rarity of the moment.

Wen and Pepe moved quietly back toward the entrance of the cave.

Pepe's expression was thoughtful as a new understanding struck him. "So that's why that wolf attacked the bear. She was protecting her pups!"

"Maybe that's why she left them by themselves in the cave," Wen added. "She heard the bear in the area."

Pepe glanced back at the pups, hesitant and concerned. "I don't think the forest service knows about this den."

Wen swallowed the lump in his throat. "What if the mother doesn't come back? She's out in the storm right now."

"We need to tell the others," Pepe said. "I'm worried about what might happen if the pups are left alone for too long."

"We have to find Tae-Song and Gina," Wen said.

Chapter 9

Bird's-Eye View

Wen peered out of the cave's entrance. He waited for the next sound of thunder, which didn't sound nearly as loud as before. It softly rumbled far off in the distance, no longer the sharp, ringing boom they had heard earlier. He glanced at Pepe, who was scanning the area for signs of Tae-Song and Gina.

"The storm's beginning to move away," said Wen.

Pepe agreed. "It's been awhile since we've seen lightning. It's almost safe to go out."

They waited, watching the sky until, with the same sudden manner with which it had appeared, the storm passed. The rain suddenly came to a stop, and the sound of thunder was a distant memory.

The two boys stepped out of the cave and splashed right into a soggy mud puddle.

Once outside, the radio in Pepe's hand began working again. The static was replaced by Gina's worried voice. "Wen? Pepe? Are you there?"

Pepe immediately responded, "Gina! Where are you?"

Gina sounded relieved. "I'm not sure. Tae-Song and I found cover under the ledge of a cliff. But Tae-Song is hurt. A branch fell on his leg, and he needs help. It might be broken." Her voice rose in a slightly panicked tone, "And I'm not sure where we are!"

Wen thought quickly and replied, "Don't worry. Pepe and I must be nearby. Tell me what you see."

"We're under a short ledge in the side of the cliff. There's a group of trees, about ten of them." Gina hesitated, then went on, "And there's a big rock nearby. I don't know what else to tell you!"

"Don't worry," Wen soothed. "We'll figure this out. Check out the trees. What do they look like?"

She said the trees had white bark and only a few branches, which meant that they were aspen trees. Then Wen asked, "What does that big rock look like?"

Gina sounded confused. "Look like? I don't know, a big egg?"

Wen smiled in triumph. "An egg with a big crack in it?"

"Yes!" Gina exclaimed. "How did you know?"

"We've passed that rock and that group of aspen trees before. I remember thinking that rock would make a good climbing rock."

Pepe clapped Wen on the back excitedly. "Way to go!"

Wen said into the radio, "I think I know where you are. Don't worry. We'll be right there."

After signing off with Gina, Wen studied their surroundings and frowned. "We've never been over here before, Pepe. I don't recognize anything. But we must be near the path, since we didn't run that far." He eyed a tall tree in front of him. It had lots of low branches, perfect for climbing.

Pepe said, "The quickest way to figure out where we are is to get a bird's-eye view."

Wen pointed up into the tree. "That means we need to climb up and see if we recognize anything."

Pepe nodded. "No problem. I'll do it."

"But you're afraid of heights," said Wen.

Pepe shrugged. "Yeah, but I'm the better climber."

He climbed the first branch, then the next, and the next. Wen could tell by the way he gripped the tree's trunk that he was afraid, but he was very brave as well. Pepe climbed up a few more branches until he was lost among the leaves. A few moments later, he gave a triumphant yell.

"I see the path! It's directly north of here!"

"North? Do you see a rotting log in the shape of an old castle?"

"Yes! I see it!"

Wen knew exactly where they were. In the last few days, he'd purposefully named parts of the path in order to remember where he had found different items of interest. The log in the shape of a castle was one of Wen's landmarks.

"Um, Wen?" Pepe called. He clung to the tree trunk as tightly as he could. "Can I come down now?"

With Pepe safely back on the ground, the two boys headed north along the path. Wen explained as they went, "All we have to do is follow this path to where I found the wild strawberry bush, then on to the group of aspen trees and the large rock with a crack in it."

They hurried along, taking the route Wen described. They found the strawberries, the group of aspen trees, the large rock, and finally, Gina and Tae-Song.

Gina was crouching next to Tae-Song, who looked dazed but awake. His ankle was propped up on a backpack. It looked sprained, but not broken.

"You found us!" Gina cried, giving both of the boys a big hug.

Pepe smiled at Wen, "We have Wen to thank."

Wen chuckled. "No, we have Pepe to thank!"

Chapter 10

The Search

The radio let out a squawk, and Jing's worried voice came over the line. "Tae-Song? Are you there?"

Tae-Song grabbed the radio, reassuring her that they were all right. Then he passed the radio to Wen. "I guess you'd better give your mom directions, since you seem to know where we are."

Wen told her everything, glad to have contact with his mother and to be able to guide them. Behind him, Pepe was telling Tae-Song and Gina their tale of the wolf den.

A few minutes later, Luis, Josephine, and Jing joined them. Pepe retold the wolf-den story, answering questions as Luis wrapped Tae-Song's ankle in a splint. Pepe helped his father make a crutch out of a broken branch.

Everyone was concerned for the health of the mother wolf. They all agreed that Josephine would help Tae-Song get back to camp, while the kids led Luis and Jing back to the spot of the fallen wolf.

They hurried to the place of the bear attack, approaching the area with caution and fear of what they might find. When they'd last seen her, the wolf had looked badly injured. With the violent storm, it was unlikely she had gotten any better.

When they arrived at the spot, it was empty. Wen was confused. What had happened? They searched the area, but the storm had washed away any tracks that might have given a clue as to what had happened to the mother wolf.

Wen, considering the situation, pointed into the trees. "She must've gone into the woods for protection from the storm. I bet she headed back to her den."

This made sense, so with directions from Wen, they closely followed the path Wen and Pepe had made in their dash from the storm. The winds had caused a great deal of damage. Branches had to be pushed aside, and it was difficult picking their way through.

They soon came across the tree Pepe had climbed, and then they found the den itself.

Luis went inside. The pups were still asleep, but the wolf mother was not with them. Jing and Gina went inside to peek at the cubs while everyone else began looking for the injured wolf.

Wen searched through the woods just south of the den. At first he didn't find anything. Then, walking around a fallen tree, he saw a large mass of damp, white fur lying still on the ground.

Wen's breath caught in his throat. The mother wolf lay several feet away, nearly hidden behind the fallen tree. It was such a shock to see her that at first he could not speak or move. She was larger than he remembered, and her coat shone white against the muddy ground. Her eyes and mouth were closed, but Wen remembered the sight of her sharp teeth and jaws as she had attacked the bear.

Afraid of waking her, Wen quietly waved to the others, his eyes fixed on the gentle rise and fall of the wolf's breathing.

Luis slowly approached the wolf. She remained unconscious, even while being looked over. Luis opened his medical kit and began examining his second patient of the day. He pulled out a syringe and gave the wolf a shot. "It's something that will keep her resting," he explained. "It won't hurt her."

He listened to her heart with a stethoscope, flashed a light in her eyes, and felt all around the wound the bear had given her. Using great care, he stitched up the wound, then wrapped it in a bandage. He was quiet the whole time, which made Wen worry even more.

Finally he looked up and gave them a smile. "There. She's lost some blood, but no major harm was done. I think she'll be okay. She's sleeping now, and when she wakes, she'll go back to her pups in the den."

Chapter 11

The Black Bear Pack

Over the next few days, until the end of the trip, every minute was full of new and wondrous observations of the puppies and their mother. The father wolf returned to the den after a couple of days. He was a large, black wolf with an intense gaze, who paced and lounged near the mouth of the den. The mother recovered nicely and was soon seen outside, playing with the puppies.

They named the new wolf pack the Black Bear Pack, in honor of the mother's daring fight with the black bear. There were no other signs of the bear, who must have decided to stay away from the area.

Wen continued to be the key observer. The group recognized Wen's particular skill for noting the details and events most of them missed.

However, all adventures must end, and, much too soon, Wen found himself folding up his tent and wondering when he would have an opportunity to use it again. He gazed around the now familiar campsite, saddened to see it slowly being reclaimed by the forest as their equipment and gear were packed and loaded up.

Jing walked over and gave Wen a hug. "This was quite an adventure, don't you think?"

Wen grinned back. "It sure was. Can we do it again?"

Jing laughed. "You were really great, you know that?"

Wen nodded. He finally understood how useful he could be. He was definitely one of the pack.

"Well, he did have some help," Gina said with a sly smile.

"He was lucky to have us on his team," Pepe added.

"You're absolutely right," Wen laughed, giving both his new friends a high-five.

"Hey, we never gave ourselves a name," Gina said. "What should we call ourselves?"

Wen thought for a minute, then lifted his water bottle and said, "Here's to the Storm Pack!"

The Storm Pack